Labor Day: Celebrating Workers, Honoring History, Shaping the Future

Liam Wilde

Published by Earthwise Press, 2023.

While every precaution has been taken in the preparation of this book, the publisher assumes no responsibility for errors or omissions, or for damages resulting from the use of the information contained herein.

LABOR DAY: CELEBRATING WORKERS, HONORING HISTORY, SHAPING THE FUTURE

First edition. September 4, 2023.

ISBN: 979-8223475941

Written by Liam Wilde.

Table of Contents

Chapter 1: Labor Day Origins

In the closing decades of the 19th century, the United States stood on the cusp of a profound transformation. The Industrial Revolution was sweeping across the nation, ushering in an era of technological innovation and economic growth. Yet, beneath the clattering machines and the rising smokestacks, a new social force was emerging—the American labor movement.

Late 19th-Century Labor Movement

The late 19th century in the United States was marked by rapid industrialization, urbanization, and the expansion of manufacturing. As factories sprang up, cities grew, and the nation's economic engine roared to life, so too did the American workforce. However, this era was not just defined by the clatter of machinery and the allure of progress; it was also characterized by harsh working conditions, grueling hours, and the absence of workers' rights.

It was in this crucible of industrialization that the labor movement took shape. Workers, often toiling for 12 hours or more a day, six or even seven days a week, began to voice their discontent. Unsafe workplaces, meager wages, and the exploitation of child labor were all too common. The workers' call for better conditions, fair wages, and improved labor rights reverberated across the nation.

Demand for a Holiday to Honor Workers

Amidst these tumultuous times, a groundswell of support emerged for a holiday dedicated to workers. Labor unions, workers' associations, and leaders within the labor movement recognized the need for a day that would honor the contributions of the American worker and acknowledge their struggles.

Peter J. McGuire, a prominent labor union leader and co-founder of the American Federation of Labor, stands out as one of the champions of this cause. McGuire envisioned a national labor holiday that would serve as a unifying force, bringing workers from various backgrounds together to celebrate their collective achievements.

Simultaneously, Matthew Maguire, a machinist and secretary of the Central Labor Union in New York, also lent his support to the idea of a national labor holiday. Both men recognized that such a holiday could draw attention to the plight of workers and the urgent need for labor reform.

Events Leading to the Establishment of Labor Day

The momentum for a national labor holiday continued to grow throughout the early 1880s. Workers and labor unions across the country organized strikes, rallies, and public demonstrations to raise awareness of labor issues and advocate for better working conditions. These actions were not only a testament to the collective power of the American workforce but also a clarion call for change.

Dedicated to Labor Day,

In recognition of the countless workers whose tireless efforts have shaped our world, this book is dedicated to the spirit of Labor Day. May this day continue to stand as a symbol of your dedication, resilience, and unwavering commitment to progress. Your labor has built nations, bridged divides, and illuminated the path towards a brighter future for all. On this day, we honor and celebrate you, the heartbeat of our society.

With gratitude and solidarity,

Liam Wilde

The first seeds of Labor Day had been sown, and they would soon bear fruit in the form of a historic celebration that marked the birth of this enduring holiday.

Historical Context and Significance of the First Labor Day Celebration

On September 5, 1882, the first Labor Day celebration took place in New York City. This momentous event signaled a turning point in the labor movement and the fight for workers' rights. Thousands of workers, representing a wide array of trades and professions, participated in a grand parade that stretched through the city streets.

Yet, this inaugural Labor Day was not merely a spectacle of workers' unity; it served as a platform for public discourse on labor issues. The day featured speeches, rallies, and gatherings that drew attention to the challenges faced by workers, the need for labor reform, and the pivotal role of the labor movement in addressing these issues.

The significance of this first Labor Day celebration extended beyond the festivities. The choice of September for this holiday was strategic—it fell between Independence Day and Thanksgiving, symbolizing the essential role of laborers in the nation's progress and prosperity.

In essence, the first Labor Day celebration encapsulated the ideals and aspirations of the labor movement. It was a day dedicated to acknowledging the struggles of the working class, demanding better conditions and fair wages, and celebrating the spirit of unity among laborers. This historic event laid the foundation for the official recognition of Labor Day as a federal holiday in 1894, establishing it as a day to honor the American worker and their invaluable contributions to the nation's growth and prosperity.

Chapter 2: The Haymarket Affair

In the annals of American labor history, the Haymarket Affair of 1886 stands as a pivotal moment—a moment marred by violence but one that would leave an indelible mark on the labor movement and the eventual creation of Labor Day.

The Haymarket Riot: A Fateful Day

On the evening of May 4, 1886, in Haymarket Square, Chicago, what began as a peaceful rally in support of workers striking for an eight-hour workday took a tragic turn. As the crowd gathered to hear labor leaders speak out against oppressive working conditions, tensions escalated. The police arrived to disperse the gathering, and an unknown individual hurled a bomb at the officers.

The explosion and the ensuing chaos resulted in the deaths of several police officers and civilians, with many more injured. The Haymarket Riot sent shockwaves throughout the nation, casting a dark shadow over the labor movement.

Labor Movement's Involvement and Goals

The labor movement was deeply entwined with the events at Haymarket Square. At the time, labor unions and workers' organizations were at the forefront of the fight for workers' rights, including the demand for an eight-hour workday. The rally in Haymarket Square was organized by labor leaders and activists sympathetic to this cause.

The labor movement's goals were clear: to secure better working conditions, fair wages, and a more humane workday for laborers. The demand for an eight-hour workday symbolized the broader struggle for workers' rights and dignity. The rallying cry, "Eight hours for work, eight hours for rest, eight hours for what we will!" embodied the aspirations of countless laborers.

Impact of the Haymarket Affair

The Haymarket Affair had a profound impact on the labor movement. In its immediate aftermath, it led to a backlash against organized labor. Authorities cracked down on labor activists, and labor leaders were arrested and charged, some unjustly. The incident fueled public fear and hostility towards the labor movement, as many viewed it as a threat to social order.

However, the Haymarket Affair also galvanized the labor movement. It became a rallying point for workers and their supporters, highlighting the sacrifices made in the fight for workers' rights. The incident served as a somber reminder of the dangers faced by those who dared to challenge the status quo.

Connection to the Creation of Labor Day

The connection between the Haymarket Affair and the eventual creation of Labor Day lies in the symbolism of the events that unfolded in Chicago in 1886. Labor leaders and activists, inspired by the sacrifice of those who lost their lives in the Haymarket Riot, continued to push for workers' rights and the recognition of their contributions.

The quest for a national labor holiday gained momentum in the wake of the Haymarket Affair. The bloodshed in Haymarket Square became a powerful symbol of the price paid by workers in their struggle for justice. It reinforced the need for a day that would honor the American worker and provide a platform for labor reform.

Chapter 3: Key Figures in Labor Day History

The journey towards the establishment of Labor Day as a national holiday was not undertaken by anonymous masses alone. It was championed by visionary leaders, tireless activists, and dedicated organizers who understood the importance of workers' rights and the need to recognize the American workforce. In this chapter, we profile some of the key figures who played pivotal roles in this historic endeavor.

Samuel Gompers: A Labor Visionary

Samuel Gompers, often regarded as one of the most influential labor leaders in American history, left an indelible mark on the labor movement and the recognition of Labor Day. Born in London in 1850, Gompers immigrated to the United States with his family as a child.

Gompers became a prominent figure in the American Federation of Labor (AFL), serving as its president for multiple terms. Under his leadership, the AFL focused on practical goals, such as higher wages, shorter workdays, and improved working conditions. Gompers' pragmatic approach helped unite various labor unions and build a cohesive labor movement.

While Samuel Gompers did not play a direct role in the initial conception of Labor Day, his relentless advocacy for workers' rights and the gradual improvements in labor conditions during his leadership of the AFL undoubtedly contributed to the broader recognition of Labor Day as a tribute to the American worker.

Peter J. McGuire: Labor's Advocate

Peter J. McGuire, often referred to as the "Father of Labor Day," was a charismatic labor union leader and co-founder of the American Federation of Labor. Born in 1852, McGuire dedicated his life to advocating for workers' rights.

It was McGuire who proposed the idea of a national labor holiday to honor the contributions of workers. He envisioned a day that would unite workers from all walks of life and provide a platform to celebrate their accomplishments. McGuire's vision and passion for the labor movement played a significant role in the eventual creation of Labor Day.

McGuire's advocacy was not limited to the concept of Labor Day; he fought tirelessly for labor reforms, fair wages, and improved working conditions. His commitment to the welfare of the American worker helped lay the groundwork for Labor Day's recognition.

Matthew Maguire: A Labor Organizer

Matthew Maguire, a machinist and labor secretary of the Central Labor Union in New York, is another figure who contributed to the establishment of Labor Day. Maguire was an active participant in the labor movement of his time, advocating for workers' rights and better working conditions.

While Maguire's role in the creation of Labor Day is often overshadowed by that of Peter J. McGuire, he nevertheless played an essential part in the labor movement. His involvement in the organization of the first Labor Day celebration in New York City in 1882 demonstrated his dedication to the cause of recognizing the American worker.

Maguire's support for the idea of a national labor holiday, along with McGuire's advocacy, helped propel the concept of Labor Day into the national spotlight. These are just a few of the key figures in labor history who championed the cause of workers' rights and contributed to the recognition of Labor Day.

Chapter 4: The Evolution of Labor Rights

The evolution of labor rights in the United States is a story of progress and struggle, marked by the gradual recognition of the fundamental rights and protections owed to the American workforce. From the earliest labor laws to the landmark legislation of the 20th century, this chapter explores the journey toward fair and equitable labor practices.

Earliest Labor Laws and Worker Protections

The early 19th century saw the emergence of the first labor laws in the United States. These laws addressed issues such as child labor, working hours, and workplace safety. Some of the earliest state-level regulations sought to limit the hours that women and children could work in factories, recognizing the need to protect vulnerable members of the workforce.

One notable example was the Massachusetts Factory Act of 1842, which limited the workday for women and children to ten hours. These early regulations laid the groundwork for future labor protections and signaled a growing awareness of the need to safeguard workers' well-being.

Development of Labor Rights Through the 20th Century

The turn of the 20th century brought significant changes to the labor landscape. Workers' demands for fair treatment and better conditions gained momentum, leading to pivotal moments such as the Triangle Shirtwaist Factory fire in 1911, which highlighted the need for improved workplace safety.

As the labor movement continued to grow, so did the push for comprehensive labor legislation. The early 20th century saw the establishment of labor unions, such as the American Federation of Labor (AFL), which advocated for workers' rights and better working conditions. These efforts culminated in the passage of the National Labor Relations Act (NLRA) in 1935, also known as the Wagner Act, which guaranteed workers the right to organize and collectively bargain.

Key Legislation: The Fair Labor Standards Act

One of the most transformative pieces of labor legislation was the Fair Labor Standards Act (FLSA) of 1938. This landmark law established a minimum wage, maximum working hours, and regulations concerning child labor. The FLSA aimed to ensure that workers received fair compensation for their labor and protection from exploitation.

Under the FLSA, the standard workweek was set at 40 hours, and overtime pay was introduced for hours worked beyond that threshold. The minimum wage provisions of the FLSA sought to prevent the exploitation of low-wage workers and promote a decent standard of living.

Shaping the Modern Labor Landscape

The laws and regulations developed throughout the 20th century fundamentally reshaped the modern labor landscape. They established a framework for workers' rights, collective bargaining, and fair compensation that continues to shape the employment landscape today.

These laws not only improved the working conditions and economic prospects of American workers but also paved the way for the creation of Labor Day as a national holiday. The recognition of Labor Day in 1894 was a testament to the growing awareness of the importance of honoring workers and acknowledging their contributions to the nation's prosperity.

Chapter 5: The Symbolism of Labor Day

Labor Day, celebrated on the first Monday in September, carries profound symbolism that transcends its status as a long weekend or the unofficial end of summer. In this chapter, we delve into the significance of this chosen date and the broader symbolism of Labor Day, which encapsulates both the triumphs and tribulations of the American workforce.

Choosing the First Monday in September

The selection of the first Monday in September for Labor Day is not arbitrary but laden with meaning. Placed strategically between Independence Day (July 4th) and Thanksgiving (late November), this date symbolizes the central role of laborers in the nation's progress and prosperity.

Independence Day celebrates the birth of the United States and the ideals of freedom and democracy. By positioning Labor Day shortly after this momentous occasion, it underscores the idea that the American worker is fundamental to the realization of these democratic ideals. Workers' contributions to the nation's development, economy, and strength are at the core of the American dream.

Thanksgiving, celebrated in late November, is a time of gratitude and reflection. By placing Labor Day before this holiday, it serves as a reminder of the importance of recognizing and appreciating the labor that goes into every aspect of our lives. It prompts us to acknowledge the hard work and dedication of the American workforce.

Broader Symbolism of Labor Day

Labor Day symbolizes the achievements and struggles of workers in the United States. It represents a day of rest, relaxation, and recreation—a well-deserved break from the toils of labor. But beyond that, it embodies the spirit of solidarity among workers and the acknowledgment of their indispensable role in building and sustaining the nation.

The holiday carries a message of empowerment, reminding workers of their collective strength and their capacity to bring about change. It serves as a beacon of hope for those striving for better working conditions, fair wages, and equitable treatment. Labor Day is a reminder that the American workforce has the power to shape the future and influence policies that impact their lives.

Representing Achievements and Struggles

Labor Day encapsulates both the achievements and struggles of workers. It is a day to celebrate the triumphs of the labor movement—the creation of labor unions, the passage of labor laws, and the improved working conditions that workers have fought for and won over the years.

Yet, it also serves as a solemn recognition of the challenges that persist. While much progress has been made, there are still issues such as wage inequality, workplace discrimination, and labor rights violations that demand attention. Labor Day is a call to action, a reminder that the struggle for workers' rights is ongoing and that the American worker's fight for dignity and justice continues.

Chapter 6: Celebrating with Labor Day Recipes

Labor Day is a time to relax, enjoy the company of family and friends, and savor delicious food. In this chapter, we offer a delightful selection of mouthwatering recipes, along with grilling tips, appetizers, main dishes, and desserts to make your Labor Day celebration a culinary delight. We'll also provide ideas for pairing food with beverages and creating a festive atmosphere.

Grilling Tips for a Perfect Labor Day BBQ

Preheat the Grill: Start with a clean, preheated grill for even cooking.

Oil the Grates: Brush the grill grates with oil to prevent sticking.

Marinate: Marinating meat or vegetables adds flavor and helps keep them tender. For chicken skewers, marinate cubed chicken breast in a mixture of yogurt, lemon juice, minced garlic, and your favorite spices.

Use the Two-Zone Method: Create hot and cool zones on the grill for searing and indirect cooking.

Let Meat Rest: Allow grilled meats to rest for a few minutes before slicing for juicier results.

Appetizers:

1. **Grilled Veggie Skewers:**

Ingredients: Bell peppers, zucchini, cherry tomatoes, mushrooms, onions.

Season with olive oil, minced garlic, fresh herbs (like rosemary and thyme), salt, and pepper. Grill until tender.

2. Caprese Salad Bites:

Ingredients: Cherry tomatoes, fresh mozzarella balls, basil leaves.

Drizzle with balsamic glaze and extra-virgin olive oil. Skewer them for easy serving.

Main Dishes:

3. Classic Burgers:

Ingredients: Ground beef or plant-based patties.

Top with lettuce, tomato slices, red onion rings, and your favorite condiments (ketchup, mustard, mayo).

4. Grilled Chicken Skewers:

Ingredients: Cubed chicken breast marinated in a mixture of Greek yogurt, lemon juice, minced garlic, paprika, cumin, and salt.

Grill until the chicken is cooked through and has a slight char.

5. BBQ Pulled Pork Sandwiches:

Ingredients: Slow-cooked pulled pork in your favorite barbecue sauce.

Serve on hamburger buns with coleslaw for a satisfying sandwich.

Desserts:

6. Fresh Fruit Salad:

Ingredients: Assorted fresh fruits like watermelon cubes, strawberries, blueberries, and pineapple chunks.

Toss with a drizzle of honey and garnish with fresh mint leaves.

7. Ice Cream Sundae Bar:

Set up a self-serve station with vanilla ice cream and an array of toppings, including chocolate sauce, caramel, whipped cream, chopped nuts, and maraschino cherries.

Beverage Pairings:

8. Classic Lemonade:

Ingredients: Freshly squeezed lemon juice, sugar, and water.

Mix to taste for a refreshing, tangy drink that pairs well with grilled foods.

9. Iced Tea:

Ingredients: Brewed tea (black, green, or herbal), ice cubes, and optional sweetener.

Offer both sweetened and unsweetened versions to cater to different preferences.

10. **Craft Beer or Wine**: - Provide a selection of craft beers or wines to complement different dishes. Consider lighter beers for burgers and grilled chicken and red wine for heartier barbecue fare.

Creating a Festive Atmosphere:

Decorate with Flags: Use American flags, patriotic bunting, and red, white, and blue tableware to add a festive touch.

Outdoor Games: Set up games like cornhole, badminton, or a water balloon toss to keep guests entertained.

Music Playlist: Create a playlist of upbeat songs, including classic rock, country, and pop, to keep the atmosphere lively.

Fireworks: If allowed in your area, end the day with a dazzling fireworks display to create a memorable finale to your Labor Day celebration.

With these recipes, tips, and ideas, your Labor Day celebration is sure to be a culinary and festive success. Enjoy the food, the company, and the spirit of the holiday!

Chapter 7: Hosting a Labor Day Picnic

Labor Day, a time of relaxation and celebration, offers the perfect opportunity to gather with loved ones in the great outdoors. In this chapter, we'll guide you through the steps to plan and host a successful Labor Day picnic, complete with journalistic insights on location selection, invitations, guest activities, menu planning, dietary considerations, picnic games, and festive decorations.

Choosing the Perfect Picnic Location

Selecting the right location sets the stage for a memorable Labor Day picnic. Local parks with ample picnic areas, shelters, and lush green spaces offer an inviting setting for outdoor gatherings. Be sure to consider essential amenities, such as restrooms and proper trash disposal facilities, to ensure your guests' comfort.

For those fortunate enough to live near the coast, a beach picnic can be a refreshing choice. However, remember to keep an eye on the tides and consider providing shaded areas to escape the sun's rays.

If you prefer the coziness of your own space, hosting a backyard picnic at home can be a convenient and intimate option. Arrange a comfortable outdoor setting with blankets and cushions to create a welcoming atmosphere.

Invitations and Guest Activities

Sending out invitations is the first step in bringing your Labor Day picnic to life. Whether you opt for digital or traditional paper invitations, be sure to include crucial details such as the date, time, location, and any specific requests, such as bringing a dish to share.

To foster a sense of community and shared responsibility, consider organizing your picnic as a potluck. Encourage guests to contribute their favorite dishes or desserts, coordinating the menu to avoid duplications.

Beyond food, plan a variety of guest activities to keep everyone entertained. Frisbee, scavenger hunts, and nature walks are excellent choices. Don't forget to bring along board games or a deck of cards for some casual, laid-back fun.

Menu Planning and Dietary Considerations

A well-curated menu is at the heart of any successful picnic. Offering a variety of sandwiches, wraps, and salads ensures there's something for everyone. To accommodate dietary preferences, include vegetarian and vegan options in your spread.

Finger foods like chips, dips, fruit platters, and cheese and charcuterie boards make for easy, crowd-pleasing snacks. As for beverages, provide a selection that caters to different tastes, including water, iced tea, lemonade, and soda. If your group includes adults, consider offering alcoholic beverages as well.

No picnic is complete without dessert. Opt for portable treats such as cookies, brownies, and fruit salad. To add a touch of Labor Day festivity, include a themed cake or cupcakes.

In your planning, be mindful of food allergies and dietary restrictions. Checking with your guests about specific needs is a thoughtful gesture. For added convenience, label dishes with ingredients to help those with dietary concerns navigate the menu.

Picnic Games and Decorations

Picnic games and decorations can elevate the festive atmosphere of your Labor Day gathering. Organize classic picnic games like sack races, tug-of-war, or a three-legged race to spark friendly competition. Consider offering prizes for winners to add to the excitement.

To enhance the ambiance, curate a playlist of upbeat tunes that resonate with the spirit of the day. Portable Bluetooth speakers can provide the necessary soundtrack for your picnic.

Don't underestimate the impact of decorations. Incorporate patriotic colors with red, white, and blue tablecloths, napkins, and utensils. A Labor Day banner or bunting can add a festive touch to your setup.

To ensure your guests' comfort and safety, provide ample seating with blankets and cushions. Additionally, don't forget essential items like sunscreen, insect repellent, and a well-stocked first aid kit.

If your chosen location lacks natural shade, consider setting up umbrellas, pop-up canopies, or a picnic shelter to shield your guests from the sun's rays.

Chapter 8: Labor Day Travel Destinations

As Labor Day approaches, many seek the opportunity for one last summer adventure or a relaxing getaway. In this chapter, we'll suggest a variety of travel destinations that are ideal for a Labor Day getaway. We'll also highlight activities, attractions, and events unique to each location, along with information on accommodations and travel logistics to make your trip planning a breeze.

Charleston, South Carolina: Historic Charm and Southern Hospitality

Charleston's cobblestone streets and historic architecture offer a picturesque backdrop for a Labor Day escape. Explore the city's rich history through guided tours of plantations and historic homes. Savor Lowcountry cuisine at renowned restaurants, and relax on nearby beaches like Folly Beach or Isle of Palms.

Lake Tahoe, California/Nevada: Alpine Adventure and Natural Beauty

For nature enthusiasts, Lake Tahoe provides an idyllic setting. Enjoy hiking, mountain biking, and water activities during the day, and relax by the campfire at night. The lake's clear waters and surrounding mountains create a stunning backdrop for your holiday.

Bar Harbor, Maine: Coastal Serenity and Outdoor Exploration

Bar Harbor, located near Acadia National Park, offers the perfect blend of coastal charm and outdoor adventure. Explore the park's hiking trails, bike paths, and picturesque coastline. Don't miss the opportunity to savor freshly caught lobster at local seafood restaurants.

Sedona, Arizona: Red Rock Wonders and Spiritual Retreat

Sedona's stunning red rock formations draw visitors seeking both adventure and relaxation. Explore the hiking trails, take a Jeep tour through the rugged terrain, or indulge in a spa day. The area's spiritual energy has also made it a destination for wellness retreats and meditation.

Key West, Florida: Tropical Paradise and Watersports Galore

For those craving a tropical escape, Key West offers sandy beaches, clear waters, and a vibrant atmosphere. Try snorkeling, parasailing, or simply relax by the beach with a frozen key lime pie on a stick. The island's historic district offers a glimpse into its maritime past.

San Francisco, California: Cultural Riches and Iconic Landmarks

San Francisco's diverse culture and iconic landmarks make it an exciting Labor Day destination. Explore the Golden Gate Bridge, Alcatraz Island, and the lively neighborhoods of Chinatown and North Beach. Enjoy world-class dining and entertainment.

Nashville, Tennessee: Music, BBQ, and Southern Hospitality

Nashville, known as Music City, is the perfect destination for music enthusiasts and foodies alike. Experience live country music performances, tour the Country Music Hall of Fame, and savor delicious barbecue. The city's vibrant nightlife adds to the festivities.

Accommodations and Travel Logistics

Booking Accommodations: Secure your lodging well in advance, especially during holiday weekends. Options range from luxury hotels and resorts to vacation rentals and campgrounds, depending on your destination.

Transportation: Consider your preferred mode of transportation, whether it's flying, driving, or taking a train or bus. Plan your travel itinerary and make any necessary reservations.

Holiday Events: Research Labor Day events and festivals at your chosen destination. Many places host parades, concerts, and special activities during the holiday weekend.

Packing: Pack appropriately for your destination's weather and activities. Don't forget essentials like sunscreen, comfortable footwear, and any specific gear needed for outdoor adventures.

Chapter 9: Planning the Ultimate Labor Day Trip

As Labor Day approaches, the allure of a well-deserved vacation beckons. Crafting the ultimate Labor Day getaway requires meticulous planning, from budgeting and transportation logistics to packing essentials and creating a sample itinerary. In this step-by-step journalistic guide, we'll help you navigate the process, ensuring your holiday is not only memorable but also stress-free.

Step 1: Define Your Labor Day Trip Goals

Every journey begins with a purpose. Before diving into the planning process, take a moment to articulate your trip's objectives. Do you long for relaxation, seek thrilling adventures, or aspire to immerse yourself in culture and exploration? Clearly defining your goals will steer you toward the perfect destination and experiences.

Step 2: Set a Realistic Budget

Budgeting is the backbone of any successful trip. Calculate your total expenses, encompassing transportation, accommodation, dining, activities, and even a little extra for souvenirs. To ensure financial comfort throughout your vacation, be mindful of existing financial commitments and obligations.

Step 3: Choose Your Destination

The choice of destination hinges on your goals and budget. Our previous chapter (Chapter 8) offers inspiration, but thorough research is crucial. Dive into the selected location's offerings, from must-see attractions and unique activities to local events and hidden gems.

Step 4: Plan Transportation

Selecting the most suitable mode of transportation is a pivotal decision. If flying is your choice, early flight bookings can secure favorable prices. On the other hand, if you're opting for a road trip, ensure your vehicle is in prime condition, and map out your route, taking rest stops and scenic detours into account.

Step 5: Accommodation Booking

As Labor Day is a sought-after holiday weekend, booking accommodations well in advance is paramount. Choices range from luxurious hotels and cozy resorts to vacation rentals and campgrounds. The key is to find a place that fits your budget and offers convenient access to your planned activities.

Step 6: Craft a Sample Itinerary

A well-structured itinerary ensures you make the most of your holiday while allowing room for spontaneity. Begin by sketching a preliminary daily plan that outlines activities, dining, and relaxation. Flexibility is key, enabling you to adapt to unexpected discoveries.

Step 7: Pack Smartly

Efficient packing is an art form. Start with a comprehensive list that covers clothing, toiletries, medication, travel documents, electronics, and any specialized gear. Check the weather forecast to pack appropriately and prevent overpacking.

Clothing: Opt for versatile pieces that can be mixed and matched, bearing in mind the destination's climate and planned activities.

Toiletries: Pack travel-sized toiletries and essential medications. Remember items like sunscreen, insect repellent, and a compact first aid kit.

Travel Documents: Safeguard your ID, passport, visa (if applicable), travel insurance, and printed reservation confirmations.

Electronics: Organize chargers, power banks, and adapters in a designated pouch for easy access.

Luggage: Select the appropriate suitcase or backpack, considering built-in organization features for convenience.

Step 8: Sample Itinerary for a Stress-Free Holiday

Here's a sample three-day Labor Day trip itinerary to get you started:

Day 1: Arrival and Exploration

Morning: Arrive at your destination, check in, and freshen up.

Afternoon: Explore the city center or nearby attractions, such as museums or parks.

Evening: Delight in local cuisine at a recommended restaurant.

Day 2: Adventure and Exploration

Morning: Dive into outdoor adventures like hiking, biking, or water activities.

Afternoon: Discover cultural landmarks or relish scenic beauty in the vicinity.

Evening: Savor local culinary delights or immerse yourself in a cultural event or performance.

Day 3: Relaxation and Departure

Morning: Enjoy a leisurely breakfast and savor some well-deserved downtime.

Afternoon: Consider a spa visit, a leisurely scenic drive, or indulging in a cherished hobby.

Evening: Bid farewell with a memorable dinner and prepare for the journey home.

Step 9: Confirm Reservations and Check-In

As your departure date draws near, it's essential to cross-check all reservations, including flights, accommodations, and pre-booked activities. Ensure you have all required travel documents and identification ready for seamless travel.

Step 10: Departure and Enjoyment

On the day of departure, follow your planned schedule, allowing extra time for potential delays. Most importantly, embrace every moment of your Labor Day trip, knowing that meticulous planning has paved the way for a remarkable and stress-free holiday.

Chapter 10: Labor Day in Movies and Literature

Labor Day, a holiday dedicated to honoring the contributions of workers, has made its mark not only in the annals of history but also in the realm of storytelling. In this chapter, we delve into how Labor Day has been portrayed in films and literature. We'll explore notable works, characters, and themes related to Labor Day, examining the cultural impact of these representations.

The Working Class on the Silver Screen:

Film has long been a platform for exploring the lives and struggles of the working class. One notable film that delves into labor-related themes is "Modern Times" (1936), directed by and starring Charlie Chaplin. The film is a poignant satire of industrialization, automation, and the dehumanizing aspects of the modern workplace. Chaplin's iconic portrayal of a factory worker struggling to find his place in a fast-paced world speaks to the timeless issues faced by workers.

Labor Unions and Solidarity:

Literature has also provided a lens through which to examine labor and workers' rights. John Steinbeck's "The Grapes of Wrath" (1939) is a classic novel that portrays the plight of Dust Bowl migrants during the Great Depression. Through the Joad family's journey, Steinbeck explores the challenges faced by laborers, the role of labor unions, and the importance of solidarity among workers.

The Labor Movement and Social Change:

Another film that delves into the labor movement and social change is "Norma Rae" (1979), starring Sally Field. Based on a true story, the film follows the journey of a textile worker who becomes a union organizer. "Norma Rae" highlights the struggles and triumphs of workers as they seek to improve their working conditions and gain a voice in their workplace.

Labor Day as a Time for Reflection:

Labor Day often serves as a backdrop for stories that reflect on the broader themes of work, life, and societal values. In literature, one such work is "Death of a Salesman" by Arthur Miller (1949). This iconic play explores the disillusionment of a traveling salesman named Willy Loman and his quest for the American Dream. The play raises questions about the meaning of work and the impact of societal expectations on individuals.

Cultural Impact and Representation:

The portrayal of Labor Day in movies and literature has had a profound cultural impact. These stories provide a window into the challenges faced by workers and the evolution of labor rights. They shed light on issues of economic inequality, social justice, and the human cost of industrialization.

Additionally, these representations serve as a reminder of the importance of honoring and recognizing the contributions of workers. Labor Day is not just a day off; it is a day to reflect on the labor movement's history and the ongoing struggles for workers' rights.

Chapter 11: Labor Day in Pop Culture Today

In the 21st century, Labor Day continues to hold a unique place in pop culture, reflecting both its historical significance and its evolution in contemporary society. This chapter explores how Labor Day is referenced and celebrated in today's pop culture landscape, examining its presence in music, television, social media, and the internet.

1. Labor Day in Music:

Music has always been a powerful medium for capturing the spirit of a holiday, and Labor Day is no exception. Artists across genres have incorporated Labor Day themes into their songs. For example, Bruce Springsteen's "My City of Ruins" pays homage to the resilience of workers and communities, while Dolly Parton's "9 to 5" addresses the challenges of the daily grind.

2. Labor Day on Television:

Television often features Labor Day-themed episodes in various series, addressing the holiday's significance in modern life. These episodes may explore themes like work-life balance, the challenges of the modern workplace, or the importance of taking a break.

3. Labor Day in Social Media:

Social media platforms provide a space for people to share their Labor Day experiences, whether through photos of barbecues, travel adventures, or relaxation. Hashtags like #LaborDay, #LongWeekend, and #EndOfSummer trend on platforms like Instagram and Twitter as users document their holiday activities and reflect on the significance of the day.

4. Labor Day Celebrations:

Contemporary Labor Day celebrations often revolve around leisure and recreation. Barbecues, picnics, and outdoor gatherings are common, with friends and family coming together to enjoy the unofficial end of summer. Parades and community events celebrate the achievements of the labor movement and workers' contributions to society.

5. Trends, Memes, and Viral Moments:

The internet has given rise to Labor Day-related trends, memes, and viral moments. Memes playfully highlight the relatable experiences of workers, from the anticipation of a long weekend to the struggle of returning to work after the holiday. Memes and viral videos often capture the humor and irony of the workweek.

6. Labor Day Sales and Shopping:

In the world of retail, Labor Day is synonymous with sales and shopping events. Stores offer discounts on a wide range of products, and online retailers promote special deals. Shoppers look forward to taking advantage of these sales as they prepare for the back-to-school season and the upcoming holidays.

7. The End of Summer:

Labor Day also marks the unofficial end of summer in the United States. Many use the long weekend as an opportunity to squeeze in one last summer vacation or outdoor adventure before cooler weather sets in.

8. Labor Day and Contemporary Issues:

In recent years, Labor Day has also become a platform for discussions on contemporary labor issues, including workers' rights, wage disparities, and the gig economy. Activists and advocates use the holiday as an opportunity to raise awareness about these challenges and advocate for change.

In the 21st century, Labor Day remains a multifaceted holiday celebrated in diverse ways. It serves as a time for relaxation, reflection, and recognition of the labor movement's historical achievements. Additionally, it continues to evolve in response to the changing nature of work and contemporary social issues, making it a relevant and dynamic part of modern pop culture.

Chapter 12: Labor Day Crafts and Decorations

Labor Day celebrations often include lively gatherings and patriotic decorations. In this chapter, we'll explore creative craft ideas for making Labor Day decorations that add a festive touch to your holiday festivities. Whether you're an experienced crafter or a beginner, these DIY projects are suitable for all skill levels. Follow the step-by-step instructions to create memorable decorations for your Labor Day celebration.

1. Red, White, and Blue Balloon Garland:

Materials:

Red, white, and blue balloons

Balloon pump

String or fishing line

Adhesive hooks

Instructions:

Inflate balloons in various sizes and colors using a balloon pump.

Tie balloons together in clusters of 3-4, mixing colors.

String the clusters onto fishing line or string, leaving a few inches of space between each.

Hang the balloon garland indoors or outdoors using adhesive hooks.

Adjust the placement and spacing as desired to create a vibrant decoration.

2. Patriotic Mason Jar Lanterns:

Materials:

Mason jars

Red, white, and blue acrylic paint

Paintbrushes

Tea light candles

Instructions:

Clean and dry the mason jars thoroughly.

Paint each jar with a base coat of either red, white, or blue paint. Allow it to dry completely.

Use paintbrushes to add patriotic designs like stars, stripes, or fireworks.

Place a tea light candle inside each jar, and light them in the evening to create a warm and inviting atmosphere.

3. Labor Day Wreath:

Materials:

Wreath form (foam or wire)

Red, white, and blue ribbon

Mini American flags

Glue gun and glue sticks

Scissors

Instructions:

Wrap the wreath form with red, white, and blue ribbon, securing it with glue as needed.

Attach mini American flags to the wreath using hot glue, spacing them evenly.

Create a bow with ribbon and attach it to the wreath as a finishing touch.

Hang the Labor Day wreath on your front door or as a centerpiece for your celebration.

4. Labor Day Table Centerpiece:

Materials:

Glass vase or jar

Mini American flags

Small white flowers (fake or real)

Red, white, and blue ribbon

Scissors

Instructions:

Fill the glass vase or jar with water.

Trim the stems of the white flowers to the desired length and arrange them in the vase.

Attach mini American flags to wooden skewers or floral wire.

Insert the flag-topped skewers or wires among the flowers.

Tie a ribbon around the vase or jar for an added patriotic touch.

Place the centerpiece on your dining table or buffet.

5. Painted Wooden Labor Day Sign:

Materials:

Wooden board or plank

Acrylic paints (red, white, and blue)

Paintbrushes

Stencils (optional)

Sandpaper

Twine or wire for hanging

Instructions:

Sand the wooden board to smooth the surface.

Paint the board with a base coat of one color (e.g., blue).

Once dry, add patriotic designs, words, or phrases using stencils or freehand painting.

Let each color dry before moving on to the next.

Attach twine or wire to the back of the sign for hanging.

Display your hand-painted Labor Day sign indoors or outdoors.

These DIY Labor Day crafts and decorations offer a fun and creative way to celebrate the holiday. Whether you choose to make balloon garlands, mason jar lanterns, wreaths, table centerpieces, or painted signs, your homemade decorations will add a festive and personalized touch to your Labor Day festivities, making them even more memorable.

Chapter 13: Handmade Labor Day Gifts

Handmade gifts are a thoughtful way to celebrate Labor Day while showing appreciation for friends and family. In this chapter, we'll provide detailed instructions for crafting unique Labor Day gifts that will leave a lasting impression. We'll also present gift ideas suitable for different recipients, and explore the special satisfaction that comes with giving and receiving handmade presents.

1. Personalized Labor Day Apron:

Materials:

Plain white apron

Fabric markers or paint

Stencils (optional)

Instructions:

Lay the apron flat on a clean surface.

Use fabric markers or paint to create Labor Day-themed designs, such as stars, flags, or the date.

You can also add a personalized touch by writing the recipient's name or a special message.

Let the design dry completely before gifting.

2. Labor Day Potpourri Sachets:

Materials:

Small fabric squares (e.g., red, white, and blue)

Dried lavender or potpourri

Ribbon or twine

Needle and thread

Instructions:

Place a small amount of dried lavender or potpourri in the center of a fabric square.

Gather the corners of the fabric square and tie them together with ribbon or twine.

Repeat the process to create multiple sachets.

You can add a small Labor Day-themed tag or label for a finishing touch.

3. Hand-Painted Labor Day Rocks:

Materials:

Smooth rocks or stones

Acrylic paints (red, white, and blue)

Paintbrushes

Varnish (optional)

Instructions:

Clean and dry the rocks thoroughly.

Use acrylic paints to create Labor Day-themed designs on the rocks, such as flags, stars, or patriotic phrases.

Allow the paint to dry completely.

For added protection and shine, you can apply a thin layer of varnish.

Arrange the painted rocks in a decorative box or bag for gifting.

4. Labor Day Memory Scrapbook:

Materials:

Blank scrapbook or photo album

Colored paper, stickers, and embellishments

Glue or double-sided tape

Photos and mementos from past Labor Day celebrations

Instructions:

Organize photos and mementos from past Labor Day celebrations.

Arrange them in the scrapbook, adding colored paper, stickers, and embellishments to create visually appealing pages.

Write captions or notes to accompany the photos, sharing memories and stories.

Present the completed scrapbook as a heartfelt Labor Day gift.

5. Handcrafted Labor Day Cards:

Materials:

Cardstock or blank cards

Colored pencils, markers, or watercolors

Labor Day-themed rubber stamps and ink pads (optional)

Instructions:

Fold the cardstock in half to create a card or use pre-made blank cards.

Decorate the front of the card with Labor Day-themed artwork, such as flags, fireworks, or a "Happy Labor Day" message.

Write a heartfelt note inside the card, expressing your wishes for a joyful holiday.

The Satisfaction of Handmade Gifts:

Handmade Labor Day gifts offer a unique opportunity to express your creativity and thoughtfulness. The act of crafting a gift allows you to infuse it with personal touches and sentiments, making it all the more meaningful for both the giver and the recipient. Handmade gifts are a way to show appreciation, celebrate the holiday, and create lasting memories with loved ones.

When you give a handmade Labor Day gift, you're not only offering a physical item but also a piece of yourself. It's a gesture that speaks to the labor of love and care you put into crafting something special, embodying the spirit of the holiday itself.

Chapter 14: Achieving Work-Life Balance

In a world where the demands of work and life can often feel overwhelming, achieving work-life balance is a vital pursuit. In this chapter, we will explore the concept of work-life balance, its significance, and offer practical strategies for maintaining equilibrium in your life. Additionally, we will discuss the role of Labor Day in promoting and emphasizing the importance of work-life balance.

Understanding Work-Life Balance:

Work-life balance refers to the equilibrium between the demands of your job and your personal life. It is a state in which you can effectively manage your career while also nurturing your well-being, relationships, and personal interests. Striking the right balance is essential for overall happiness and fulfillment.

The Importance of Work-Life Balance

Achieving work-life balance is crucial for several reasons:

Physical and Mental Health: Balancing work and life reduces stress, anxiety, and the risk of burnout, leading to improved overall health.

Enhanced Productivity: When you prioritize self-care and personal time, you return to work with increased energy and focus, leading to higher productivity.

Stronger Relationships: Investing time in your personal life fosters healthier relationships with family and friends.

Personal Growth: Pursuing hobbies and interests outside of work promotes personal growth and development.

Practical Strategies for Achieving Balance

Set Boundaries: Clearly define your work hours and personal time. Avoid overextending yourself or consistently bringing work home.

Prioritize Self-Care: Make self-care a non-negotiable part of your routine. This can include exercise, meditation, hobbies, or simply downtime.

Delegate and Ask for Help: Don't hesitate to delegate tasks at work or ask for assistance in your personal life when needed.

Time Management: Use effective time management techniques, such as the Pomodoro Technique, to maintain focus at work and create time for leisure.

Unplug: Disconnect from work emails and notifications when you're off the clock to avoid constant work-related stress.

Set Goals: Define both professional and personal goals to help you stay motivated and on track.

Labor Day's Role in Promoting Balance

Labor Day serves as a poignant reminder of the importance of work-life balance. It was established to honor the contributions of workers and the labor movement, emphasizing the value of workers' rights and well-being. By taking a day off on Labor Day, you are symbolically recognizing the need for rest and rejuvenation, a critical component of work-life balance.

In contemporary society, Labor Day encourages people to step back from their busy routines, spend quality time with loved ones, and recharge. It serves as a reminder that work is a means to an end – a way to support and enrich our lives, rather than dominating them.

Chapter 15: Labor Day Reflections

Labor Day is not just a day for picnics and parades; it's also an opportunity to reflect on the significance of work, the labor movement, and our own careers and lives. In this chapter, we will collect and share personal stories and anecdotes about the importance of Labor Day. We'll encourage readers to engage in self-reflection, discussing how Labor Day can serve as a time for introspection and goal-setting.

Personal Stories and Anecdotes

Story 1: The Generations of Labor Sarah, a third-generation factory worker, reflects on how Labor Day gatherings were an annual tradition in her family. It was a day to celebrate their hard work and the progress made by workers in their industry. The stories shared around the picnic table served as a reminder of the sacrifices and achievements of previous generations.

Story 2: A Career Transformation John shares his journey from a high-stress corporate job to a fulfilling career as a freelance writer. Labor Day marked the turning point when he decided to prioritize his passion for writing and seek a better work-life balance. It's a reminder that sometimes, a shift in perspective can lead to profound changes in one's life.

Story 3: A Tribute to Essential Workers During the height of the COVID-19 pandemic, Maria worked as a nurse in a busy hospital. She reflects on how Labor Day took on new meaning as a day to honor essential workers. It was a time to acknowledge the sacrifices and dedication of those on the frontlines, often at great personal risk.

Encouraging Reflection

Assess Your Career: Take a moment to evaluate your current career path. Are you satisfied with your work? Are there changes you'd like to make? Labor Day can serve as a checkpoint for career reflection.

Recognize Achievements: Celebrate your professional accomplishments, no matter how big or small. Reflect on the skills you've developed and the challenges you've overcome.

Set Goals: Use Labor Day as an opportunity to set new career and life goals. What do you aspire to achieve in the coming year? Setting goals can provide direction and motivation.

Balance Check: Evaluate your work-life balance. Are you dedicating enough time to personal pursuits, relationships, and self-care? If not, consider adjustments.

Gratitude: Express gratitude for the opportunities you've had in your career. Labor Day is an ideal time to acknowledge the support of colleagues, mentors, and loved ones.

Labor Day as a Time for Goal-Setting

Labor Day's position at the end of summer and the beginning of the fall season makes it an excellent time for goal-setting. Just as students return to school with renewed focus, adults can use this holiday as a fresh start to reevaluate and revitalize their professional and personal aspirations.

Whether it's pursuing a new career path, seeking a better work-life balance, or dedicating time to personal growth, Labor Day can serve as a catalyst for positive change. By reflecting on the significance of the holiday and its connection to work, we can set meaningful goals and strive for a more fulfilling life.

Chapter 16: Labor Day Around the World

While the United States has its own celebrated Labor Day, similar holidays and traditions exist around the world. In this chapter, we'll take readers on a global tour of Labor Day and similar observances, shedding light on unique customs and traditions in various countries. We'll compare and contrast international celebrations with the U.S. holiday, showcasing the diversity of approaches to honoring workers and labor movements.

International Workers' Day (May Day)

Location: Global, including countries like the United Kingdom, Germany, Russia, and Brazil.

Traditions: International Workers' Day, often referred to as May Day, typically involves labor unions, workers' demonstrations, and parades. In some countries, it's a day for political rallies and protests, while in others, it's a festive occasion with dances, music, and cultural events. The day serves as a reminder of the labor movement's global impact.

Labour Day (Canada)

Location: Canada

Traditions: Similar to the United States, Canada celebrates Labour Day on the first Monday in September. It's a day for picnics, parades, and outdoor activities. Canadians also mark the end of summer with this holiday, enjoying the last long weekend before the fall season.

International Workers' Day (India)

Location: India

Traditions: In India, International Workers' Day is known as "Antarrashtriya Shramik Diwas." It's a time to acknowledge the struggles and achievements of the labor movement. Various trade unions organize rallies and events, highlighting workers' rights and welfare.

Labour Day (Australia)

Location: Australia

Traditions: Australians celebrate Labour Day on different dates depending on the state, but it's typically held in October. It's a day for family outings, parades, and community events. The holiday commemorates workers' efforts to secure better working conditions and reasonable working hours.

Golden Week (China)

Location: China

Traditions: While not directly related to Labor Day, China's Golden Week includes the Labor Day holiday. This week-long national holiday is marked by travel, shopping, and tourism. Many Chinese workers take advantage of the time off to explore their country or travel abroad.

Fête du Travail (France)

Location: France

Traditions: Fête du Travail is celebrated on May 1st in France with parades, marches, and demonstrations. It's also customary to offer lily-of-the-valley flowers to loved ones as a symbol of good luck and solidarity.

Comparing International Celebrations

International Labor Day celebrations often share common themes of honoring workers, advocating for workers' rights, and promoting unity among laborers. However, each country adds its own unique cultural elements and historical context to the holiday.

In the United States, Labor Day is a blend of honoring workers and celebrating the end of summer. It's marked by picnics, barbecues, and outdoor leisure.

In contrast, International Workers' Day in many countries carries a stronger political and historical message, emphasizing the labor movement's achievements and the ongoing struggle for workers' rights.

Chapter 17: Labor Day and Workers' Rights Today

As Labor Day approaches each year, it serves as a reminder of the ongoing challenges and triumphs in the realm of workers' rights and labor activism. In this chapter, we'll explore the current landscape of labor-related social issues and challenges. We'll also discuss contemporary advocacy for workers' rights and workplace equality, shedding light on recent developments and trends in labor activism.

Current Labor-Related Social Issues

Workers' Rights in the Gig Economy: The rise of the gig economy has led to debates about worker classification and labor protections. Many gig workers lack traditional benefits and job security.

Income Inequality: Income inequality remains a pressing issue, with a growing wealth gap between workers and corporate executives. Calls for fair wages and wealth redistribution continue.

Workplace Equality: The fight for workplace equality encompasses gender pay gaps, discrimination, and harassment issues. Organizations and movements like #MeToo advocate for safer, more equitable work environments.

Labor Unions and Collective Bargaining: Labor unions are adapting to new industries and technologies, seeking to protect workers' rights and secure better conditions for their members.

Remote Work and Telecommuting: The COVID-19 pandemic accelerated the shift toward remote work, raising questions about work-life balance, remote worker protections, and the future of office culture.

Contemporary Advocacy for Workers' Rights:

Fight for $15: The Fight for $15 movement advocates for a higher federal minimum wage of $15 per hour. It has gained momentum in various states and municipalities.

Worker Co-operatives: The promotion of worker co-operatives, where employees collectively own and manage their workplaces, has gained attention as a way to empower workers and create more equitable businesses.

Labor Organizing: Workers in various industries, from tech to healthcare, are increasingly engaging in labor organizing efforts to address workplace issues and secure better conditions.

Remote Worker Rights: Advocacy for remote worker rights focuses on issues like fair pay, cybersecurity, and the right to disconnect from work outside of scheduled hours.

Recent Developments and Trends:

COVID-19 Impact: The pandemic brought attention to essential workers' contributions and highlighted issues such as workplace safety, paid sick leave, and healthcare access.

Hybrid Work Models: As companies adopt hybrid work models, labor activists are negotiating new terms, including remote work policies and flexible scheduling.

Climate and Labor: Climate activism and labor movements are increasingly intersecting, as workers in environmentally impactful industries seek just transitions and sustainable employment.

Digital Activism: Labor activists are using social media and online platforms to mobilize workers, share stories, and raise awareness about workplace issues.

Global Labor Solidarity: International labor movements are collaborating to address issues like global supply chain labor conditions and corporate accountability.

Chapter 18: The Gig Economy and Labor Day

The gig economy, characterized by short-term, freelance, and independent work arrangements, has reshaped the landscape of modern labor. In this chapter, we will examine the impact of the gig economy on contemporary labor dynamics and explore how Labor Day relates to the changing nature of work. Additionally, we will analyze the gig economy's implications for workers' rights and the ongoing struggle for labor justice.

The Gig Economy's Impact on Modern Labor

Flexibility vs. Precarity: Gig work offers flexibility but often comes with job insecurity, lack of benefits, and inconsistent income. Workers may find themselves in precarious situations without job stability.

Worker Classification: The debate over whether gig workers should be classified as independent contractors or employees has legal and financial implications, affecting benefits and labor protections.

Income Inequality: Gig work can contribute to income inequality, as high-earning gig workers coexist with those struggling to make ends meet.

Labor Day and the Changing Nature of Work

Historical Significance: Labor Day's origins are rooted in the labor movement's fight for workers' rights and recognition. It's a day to honor the contributions of all workers, including those in the gig economy.

Reflection on Progress: Labor Day provides an opportunity to reflect on the progress made in workers' rights and to consider how the changing nature of work impacts labor dynamics.

Advocacy for Gig Workers: Labor activists use Labor Day as a platform to advocate for gig workers' rights, pushing for fair wages, benefits, and protections.

Implications for Workers' Rights

Benefits and Protections: Gig workers often lack access to essential benefits such as health insurance, paid leave, and retirement plans. Advocacy efforts seek to secure these rights for gig workers.

Collective Bargaining: The gig economy challenges traditional collective bargaining models. Workers and organizations are exploring alternative approaches to represent gig workers' interests.

Regulatory Changes: Policymakers are considering regulatory changes to address gig worker classification and labor protections, aiming to strike a balance between flexibility and security.

Chapter 19: Labor Day's Future

As we look to the future, Labor Day stands at a crossroads, reflecting the evolving landscape of work, labor activism, and the global economy. In this chapter, we will speculate on the future of Labor Day and the labor movement, discussing emerging trends, challenges, and opportunities in the world of work. We'll also encourage readers to consider the role they might play in shaping this future.

The Future of Labor Day

Relevance in a Changing World: Labor Day will continue to serve as a reminder of the historical struggles for workers' rights and the importance of recognizing labor's contributions. Its relevance may evolve to address contemporary issues and emerging labor dynamics.

Globalization: Labor Day may become a more global celebration, emphasizing the interconnectedness of workers across borders and the need for international labor solidarity.

Digital Activism: The rise of digital platforms and social media will play a significant role in shaping how Labor Day is observed and how labor activists mobilize support.

Emerging Trends in the World of Work

Remote Work and Technology: Advancements in technology will continue to impact how and where work is performed, with remote work becoming more prevalent. The challenge will be to ensure fair treatment and protections for remote and digital workers.

Automation and AI: As automation and artificial intelligence advance, discussions on the future of work will intensify, with a focus on reskilling and upskilling the workforce.

Sustainability: The intersection of labor and environmental concerns will gain prominence, with a focus on creating sustainable jobs and green industries.

Challenges and Opportunities

Workers' Rights: The struggle for workers' rights will persist, particularly for gig workers, who may seek improved labor protections and benefits.

Income Inequality: Addressing income inequality will remain a critical challenge, with calls for fair wages and wealth redistribution.

Climate and Labor: The labor movement may collaborate more closely with environmental activists to advocate for just transitions and sustainable employment.

Readers' Role in Shaping the Future:

Advocacy: Readers can become advocates for workers' rights by supporting labor unions, engaging in labor activism, and participating in movements that promote fair labor practices.

Education: Staying informed about labor issues, emerging trends, and policy changes empowers readers to make informed decisions and contribute to discussions on the future of work.

Entrepreneurship: Those with entrepreneurial ambitions can explore business models that prioritize fair labor practices and ethical employment.

Political Engagement: Voting for policies that promote workers' rights and labor justice can have a significant impact on shaping the future of work.

Chapter 20: Celebrating Labor Day Together

Labor Day is not just a holiday for rest and relaxation; it's a day for coming together as a community to celebrate the collective achievements of workers and the labor movement. In this chapter, we will emphasize the importance of celebrating Labor Day with gratitude and unity. We'll suggest ideas for community events and volunteer opportunities on Labor Day and encourage readers to connect with others and make a positive impact in their communities.

The Spirit of Gratitude and Unity

Labor Day offers a valuable opportunity to reflect on the importance of work, the contributions of workers, and the progress made in securing workers' rights. It's a day to express gratitude for the labor movement's historic victories and for the work that people do every day to make our communities and societies thrive.

Community Events and Activities

Labor Day Parades: Attend or participate in a local Labor Day parade, where unions, workers, and community organizations come together to celebrate and showcase their solidarity.

Picnics and Barbecues: Organize or join a community picnic or barbecue, complete with games, music, and delicious food. It's a great way to connect with neighbors and friends.

Labor History Exhibitions: Visit a local museum or exhibition dedicated to labor history to gain a deeper understanding of the struggles and triumphs of the labor movement.

Film Screenings: Host a screening of a documentary or film related to labor rights and workers' experiences, followed by a discussion.

Volunteer Opportunities on Labor Day:

Community Service: Participate in a community service project, such as volunteering at a local shelter, cleaning up a park, or assisting with a charity event.

Food Drives: Organize or contribute to a food drive to help those in need in your community.

Job Fairs: Support or attend a job fair to connect job seekers with potential employers, helping individuals find meaningful employment.

Labor Rights Workshops: Offer or attend workshops and seminars on workers' rights, workplace safety, and employment opportunities.

Connecting with Others:

Networking: Use Labor Day gatherings and events as opportunities to network with people in your industry or community who share your passion for workers' rights and labor justice.

Community Engagement: Get involved in local labor organizations, unions, or community groups focused on workers' issues. Your involvement can make a meaningful impact.

Support Local Businesses: Celebrate Labor Day by supporting local businesses and shops, especially those owned by workers or cooperative enterprises.

Don't miss out!

Visit the website below and you can sign up to receive emails whenever Liam Wilde publishes a new book. There's no charge and no obligation.

https://books2read.com/r/B-A-PDPY-YPSNC

BOOKS 2 READ

Connecting independent readers to independent writers.

www.ingramcontent.com/pod-product-compliance
Lightning Source LLC
Chambersburg PA
CBHW061331120726
48001CB00002B/793